How to Write Less and Profit More

A Rich Adventure in Short Read Kindle Publishing

Audio available: http://livesensical.com/go/write-less/

Table of Contents

Bonus

*Get No-Charge Access to
Writing and Publishing Materials
from Our Library Collection*

Instant Access – Join Here

Click or type into your browser:

http://livesensical.com/go/writingbooks/

Introduction

Deep in the heart of the ever-growing Amazon Kindle jungle, there's a profitable underserved market which is not easily discovered. It sits in a clearing by itself, much like a massive stone temple rising above the forest. A temple with some gold-filled rooms.

Just my kind of area to explore. I've long been in favor of "find where everyone is going and go the opposite way." So this makes a lot of sense. And any adventure is always welcome.

We saw this expedition hinted at by Steve Scott with his non-fiction habits books. But he never really explored the opportunities this area has. In re-tracing Scott's own path, it showed me the turns he *didn't* take.

That inspired me to start my own journey around two months ago. I'm currently publishing an average of one short read ebook per week. And the results are promising, as the Christmas sales influence fades.

This path struck my fancy, as it told more about how to really use short reads as a business strategy. How to cement those 6-figures that Scott started having. What I've discovered accelerates that progress, perhaps even creating your 7-figure income.

(BTW, in Scott's recent videos, he points out that his income is still dwindling, down from a high of around $400K annually to an average of "just" $250K per year. While this is still great, it also shows that he's left tons of money on the table.)

One of the more profitable avenues is in business publishing. A lot of businesses are getting into content marketing these days, but don't have a lot of thick texts sitting around waiting to be turned into Kindle ebooks.

What they do have is lots of shorter material which would be perfect how-to non fiction books about their particular industry. If these could also be quickly turned into small books to hand out at tradeshows and by their sales people, a business could get a real marketing advantage over any competition.

And such production can be fast. The book you are reading (although more work could have been done in editing, to be sure) was created and published into four widely-distributed formats in only three days, at a cost of sweat-equity only. Imagine what could be done for your next product release...

This isn't just for fiction writers. It's for everyone with a message to get out.

So let's get started...

The Secret Map to Short Read Riches

Here's the secret map - How to Succeed with Kindle Short Reads, by Geoff Shaw.

There's a growing group of readers which Amazon has been catering to with their Kindle Short Reads. Shaw describes them like this:

> *"Introducing Coffee Break Readers*
>
> *"There's a new generation of readers.*
>
> *"People who will download and read lots of books. They only have so much time and they want their fill of excitement in that limited time.*
>
> *"We call them the CBR's - the coffee break readers.*
>
> *They're not just people who have never read longer books before... They're anyone who has limited time to read for whatever reason.*
>
> *"These people aren't stuck into a certain author, it's more like the certain type of entertainment they want: short stories which they can read in their available time."*

That idea opened my eyes quite a bit.

The price range for these CBR books is the same as Scott's .99 and 2.99, plus the 3.99 or 4.99 boxed sets.

*But the trick is that you're having to write a lot **less** and profiting **more** from each bit you do write.*

When we last left our hero, Scott seemed to be getting into longer and longer books as he went, but this is the reverse of where you want to go. You'll see shortly that this is more of a pioneer territory with a lot less competition and few tools to use to find your way. What Scott should have been doing is to figure out how to multiply his success in related genres, and stick to the short reads and box sets.

It's really all the "deep backbench" principle again. The more books you have up there, the more they can be recommended, the more chances you have to uncovered your room of gold.

Less Competition, More Profits

The great part is that this is still mostly virgin wilderness. Go look over Amazon short reads and you'll see there is a lot less competition, as the books are split up by length as well as genre. People can have 15, 30, 45, 60, and 90-minute reads. Your book still shows up in the regular categories. but the CBR's will specifically hunt up your books according to the time they have to read. So it's easier for them to find your books.

Basically, Amazon counts every 250 words as a page. Except for special instances, they generally only accept 2500-word books these days. So Shaw's chart shows the reading time category you'll fall into with your short reads, depending on word count.

Let's look at that competition you *won't* have:

For instance:

> **Literature & Fiction -**
> *Kindle Books:* 1,352,061
> *Kindle Short Reads (30 min):* 48,093
>
> **Business & Money -**
> *Kindle Books:* 249,574
> *Kindle Short Reads (30 min):* 15,937

Which arena would you like to compete in?

Another point is that there's higher turnover. People are basically consuming books like tasty snacks. This then leverages your writing far beyond anything we've seen before. They aren't looking for books they can read a bit of each day (munching all week long) but rather 5-10 books they can finish each week.

For the money they'd spend buying a traditionally-published big name author's ebook, they can buy just as much reading material for less than half - and it's all designed to be read in those tiny snippets of time they have available.

Shaw says that the bulk of the reads in this category are actually indie authors, so this means the Big 5 publishing houses won't compete with their big promotion budgets in this arena.

Shaw points out, as I did earlier, that you can publish a single 80,000-word book and take a month writing it. (And another month editing and proofing it.)

Or – write eight 10,000-word books and publish every two weeks. (One for writing at 2,000 per day - 10,000 words - and the next week for editing/proofing.)

In two months, the first author has one book, which will sell for 4.99 or so.

The second author has 8 books that can sell at 2.99.

The second author has twice the royalties coming in, plus:

- the ability to get readers as email subscribers also from each *additional* book (with a Lead Magnet at both beginning and end)
- the ability to be searched for 56 keywords and in 16 categories, instead of just 7 keywords and 2 categories.
- the greater number of his books and his more frequent releases prompt Amazon to recommend these other titles.
- and you're making income *while* you are writing.
- *then* creating a box set of these (or even a couple) just adds to the above.

In this hypothetical match-up, you have the same amount of words for each author, a tiny bit more overhead in producing covers and descriptions for short reads each ebook, plus building that box set. But then the box set allows a longer-read customer to consume the full novel.

As a sidebar, the box set looks to be a better bargain than the 80,000-word single book. Would you rather buy a collection of 8 books for 4.99 or a single book for 4.99?

This starts to point out the factors in Steve Scott's system that he was missing.

What you've also done is to create 9 books (8 singles, plus the box set) in the same amount of time as the other author, but on your author page, you've got 9 books they can check out (and buy). And that's two months' work. The audience then doesn't question if you're a one-shot wonder, but will know by the end of just two months that you're a serious contender.

The other successes I've studied spent an entire year or more creating their bigger novels in order to have 5 or 6 books available (which was Scott's average, by the way, and he was doing short books.)

Again, you can have 9 books published in just two months. Instant legitimacy, with less competition.

Setting the first ebook as perma-free is an even better option. Plus, you can give it away from your site (and also from your box set look-inside) to get their email address. You aren't giving away your first 80,000-word book (which freaks most beginning authors out) but only *1/8th* of your total work.

(One tip here is to tell them in the first line of each single book's description that a box set is also available.)

Shaw talks quite a bit about Kindle Unlimited here, but I still hold that you're throwing away income if you're not offering your works for sale everywhere possible (see Addendum.) The places you should publish in my opinion are Amazon, Itunes, and Lulu (both as an aggregator and hardcopy publisher.) This gives you the minimal interfaces to deal with.

Hook, Line, Sinker and the Lead Magnet

This is a tip Shaw gives which I've seen nowhere else: Inside your first book, it says: "Get the next book in this series!" and has a link which goes to a landing page opt-in. When they sign up, they go to a thank you page, which lists all the rest of the books in that series, as well as your other series - and they can buy each of the books through that page, directly from Amazon. That "thank you page" also has the free samples linked.

To my mind, this would be where you also give a link to sell a bundle for each ebook. It would include the PDF, epub, and mobi files as a download from your own site.

(Shaw does give a way you can help them side-load it with their Kindle email link. This builds relationship.)

Now, note that you will be building your ARC (Advance Review Copy) subscribers with your email. This segments part of them into a special list so you can sent preview copies in exchange for a review on Amazon. This is the key way to make "bestsellers" on Amazon. I did find a slightly better take on this from Mark Dawson, who has:

> a) Tell your ARC about the release date.
>
> b) Tell the rest of your list the day after, letting them know the price is going up.
>
> c) Tell your entire list the day the price is going up.
>
> d) Then (my addition) post to your blog/podcast with the release data and use IFTTT to syndicate it everywhere.
>
> e) You'd then run Facebook ads about the book, particularly if it were a boxed set, where the increased book income would pay for those ads. ($4.99 or so.)

What that does, per Dawson, is to give you immediate reviews and sales, then gets continuing sales afterwards, as Amazon will promote books which are new and continuing to sell well.

Additional Short Read Marketing Tactics

Shaw comes up with some marvelous tactics with short reads, which are just as applicable to bigger books, but not as quickly or easily done.

1) Collaborations with pen names

This tactic can be used for testing other genres, but is also essentially brand-extension. Your first pen name is known for a certain sub-genre, then you write a book in a related sub-genre adding a co-author that is actually just another pen name. It's not hard to see the cross-selling aspects of this. You can now can have several authors with their own list segment, for each sub-genre you want to write in. Shaw explains this in more detail in his course.

Your emails then come from an embracive source (like your publishing house or an "imprint" of it) which then lists the books by each author for each sub-genre. Each author could have their own special offer going.

As you segment off your hotter audience (more opens, clickthroughs) then you can give them polls, in order to narrow down what they like most and so create a better experience for them.

2) Collaborations with other (real) authors

If you have a box set with books by several of your pen names, you can then offer other authors in those sub-genres a chance to get into that box set. Since you have several "authors" already, it's a no-brainer. And that new author then emails his list about that box set. This is an old standby of affiliate marketing. It builds both your lists.

3) Cloning

For fiction short reads this is a viable option. Taking your book outline (Shaw has a course on this as well on Udemy) you then get some ghostwriters to produce another book with the same basic plot. You then publish this under that pen name. Similar cover, similar title, cloned. It works because people want more of what they love.

4) Reverse Launch

You can also release the box set first, and then offer them your first book in that series as a sample - and put that in your "Look Inside". Then you can go ahead and release the other books on a schedule, getting people to opt-in to your list to get the "early bird discount" as each new single is released.

Non-Fiction and Public Domain Publishing

Amazon is seeming to do all they can to discourage any more PD from showing up there. I got reminded this last week as I had a special report (quick read) that wound up in their very slow PD queue because of its title alone. My other books were getting approved in about 12 hours, so having to spend 5 days getting a book out of that queue back into draft was really annoying.

So I will definitely avoid this route just because it slows the speed of publishing. This also points out that they are primarily working with a database of titles (and maybe authors) as opposed to any search of submitted content (which might occur later, once it gets kicked into human hands, but that's doubtful.)

Another cross-over point is improving your writing. Writing a good non-fiction book has a great deal to do with how they write good fiction. Mainly things like having a good hook, and using emotional descriptions.

Plus, fiction is more profitable in general than non-fiction. People like to be entertained and to escape. If you can bring these same writing styles into non-fiction, then you have a popular hit.

All short-reads do is to make your books more consumable, which is the same point of learning fiction-writing techniques.

The benefit of this strategy is to enable you to get more leverage out of the same amount of content that you're going to create anyway.

Pen names to fill space in a magazine is nothing new. Prolific authors have often resorted to these for any number of reasons. Being able to cross-connect these authors and their readers gives you new opportunities for income.

I just wanted to tell you all about these, as this is a breakthrough down this line of short reads.

And authors with existing books - depending on how they are written - can break up their books into a serial format and do this same thing. The first short-read excerpt becomes a sample, then release the other chapters along this same line. Gladwell's *Tipping*

Point could have been released like this, if that were a publishing option at the time. Remember, it has to read like a serial to be successful along this line.

Leveraging Your Resources

Further, I still recommend coming out with both paperback and hardback editions to get the most out of your title. And don't forget your audio book.

Some tips came to light this last Christmas season. It turns out that Amazon will stop ordering books for certain titles if they come from Lulu or other publishers, but not their own CreateSpace (CS). You can see how this makes sense from a shipping point, but you'll also see that you just lost sales for the couple of weeks just before Chrismas. That means all the last-minute shoppers can't get your books if you don't publish to CS.

CS doesn't do hardbacks. Period. They do a lot of different cut sizes in paperback that Lulu doesn't, however. So you can make a pocketbook paperback version on CS, and a trade paperback version on Lulu, as well as a trade hardback version (both casewrap and dust-jacketed.)

Note, Amazon will show your CS version on the front page, and your Lulu version will have to be searched for. Having your expanded reach on Lulu gets your book into the other outlets with higher royalties and no Amazon stigma attached.

The general theory is this:

- You have titles which are selling as ebooks and long enough to make at least a 32-page book in print, or about 8,000 words.)

- Pocket paperback version on CS, just to Amazon.

- Trade paperback version from Lulu with their expanded reach. - Casewrap hardback from Lulu with expanded reach.

- "Deluxe" dust jacketed version at a much higher price.

Work your books backwards in order of sales so that improved title sales pays for the proofing costs of the hardcopies.

Editing itself can give you an audio book.

You have four drafts of your book. First is your rough draft. Second is cleaning up your errors and inserting links, plus general formatting. Third is reading the book out-loud and correcting anything you find. At this point, you record everything you read out loud, with attention to reading the final version into your recording. You then send off that 3rd draft to a proofer. Meanwhile, you edit your recording into shape as an audio book (or as a podcast.)

For instance. this podcast transcript is now over 4000 words in print. So it would qualify as a 30 minute quick read, but isn't big enough to print by itself. (I could add material to the end pulled from my other books, and also put in ads to buy my other books on Amazon.)

So we will probably use this as a test of this whole publishing scene

While your recording can become your audio book, it's also a podcast. Including that link into your ebook then gives you added value. I also include the link into the PDF version at the bottom as a footer. So when you submit the PDF to make your hardcopy version, they can always type that link into their browser and get the podcast.

Of course, that sends them to your podcast where they get your ads, and another way to get them into your membership/mailing list.

Quick Reads Other Than Amazon

Of course this strategy works everywhere else, too. Your ebook are the same. You don't have the "Look Inside" but all the ebook outlets enable previews - just make sure the PDF you upload has links to where you want readers to go. I'm also a fan of uploading the entire PDF, as it builds trust and encourages them to get a version they can read more easily on their smart phone. (But I do format my PDFs for 6"x9" as these are more readable on smaller screens.)

Podcasts and Keeping Updated

One final thought is to tell you to follow my Authorpreneur Flipboard magazine to keep up with all that I'm finding daily on book publishing and content creation.

I may work this up into publishing this as a weekly digest at some point, but don't know when. Let me know by return email or comment on this episode if you think that's something you could use.

This podcast was started as another self-publishing test, and it's succeeded far beyond what I expected. However, I have no need to simply work at finding more stuff to talk about just to have a podcast. I do like to share breakthroughs. But at this point, I've covered the bulk of the basics and have no reason to do like Steve Scott and others who are now trying to profit off selling courses to their list.

This is mainly as that market is *so* saturated, it's not funny. The ebook market is, frankly, glutted. The how-to books market for new authors is worse. *Amazon is more the new-author graveyard than ever before.* Most of this is because authors are following the followers rather than reaching for the top 5%. That's where the real creative energy is. Market leaders are constantly creating. And that's what makes them leaders. Everyone who tries to just copy what someone else is doing is just another also-ran.

Scott was onto something with his short reads. But he's another follower, even though well-paid. Essentially, he's always been an affiliate marketer. And that's always a follow-the-follower scene. It shows in his latest course in how to write and market books.

Any breakthrough in leveraging Amazon is in finding what are still niche areas, such as short-reads. Amazon is a complete pain to work with, as they nickel-and-dime your royalty income every chance they get. But they can be leveraged and they can be used to build your own list.

You do need your own site, and you should be able to sell your own books from your own site. I should finally have my own ecommerce site up later this month. You already see my membership site is up as a bare-bones operation, but I'm adding content to this each week. And my email lists are slowly building as I go.

Here's the minimum basics in sequence for a successful author, outside of their ability to write:

      1) an autoresponder service

      2) a domain of your own

      3) a membership on that domain

      4) your own hosted bookstore

Everything else is getting your books also offered by the main outlets so you can use those outlets to build your email subscriber lists.

If you don't have these four points above in, then you are just asking to be booted off Amazon at some point and left with no income, nothing.

The secret to profits from Amazon is to leverage their ebook sales into hardcopy sales, which are not subject to their money-grubbing policies on royalties. The real market for fiction and non-fiction, especially PD and PLR books, is in POD versions, not ebooks.

And those few comments above sum up my entire accumulated wisdom on selling books profitably. The rest is technical how-to which can be dug up just about anywhere (although the books I've already published in this area have been described as a Gold Mine with all those technical nuggets you can find inside.) My earlier books were to help anyone start with just the computer and Internet connection they already have, plus a common sense approach mostly lacking in the bulk of the other books in this area.

But I have no reason to revisit my own books. This scene is constantly shifting and evolving. I'd be forever just keeping these updated.

I'm not going to promise you that my podcast will continue. If I don't find anything really interesting, or a breakthrough, then it's just another day in the life. Frankly, these two Shaw courses on

Udemy have inspired a completely new approach for me - but there's no reason to repeat what he's already written, other than this review.

I'm also studying Mark Dawson's course on Facebook advertising, but this is a back-up to having a lot of books out there already. Your sequence would be to study the two Shaw courses and then Dawson's free videos (until his pricey FB ad course opens up once again.) If you only have a couple of nickels to invest, then get my cheaper ebooks and work on building your backlist. Once the money starts dribbling in, then invest in the above - AFTER you have your own list, domain, membership, and ecommerce set up (which can be built with just Blogger, PayPal, and MailChimp - all free to start with.)

Again, before you start publishing your books (you should always be writing, every single day) get your basics in above. Then expand your training with Shaw and Dawson. If you go back through my blog posts, I've given you other downloads to study through. All free.

Your main focus is to *thoroughly study and test everything for yourself*, then *throw away everything that doesn't work for you*. Especially what I've told you. No prophet is sacrosanct, regardless of how many followers they have or how much money they make.

Your life is your own. Live it to the fullest you can. Enjoy every moment. Listen *only* to those who have escaped that bucket of crabs where everyone else lives.

While I'm way behind and underneath my production goals these days, I still work to see how I can help you with whatever you need. Your input helps and inspires me. Email me directly or leave a comment.

And, thanks for being there.

How to Execute Short Read Publishing for Your Business

While most of this book has been written for the indie author, it has everything to do with businesses small and large.

A lot has been said about having a published book as a five-pound business card. Instant authority, instant recognition.

With short read publishing, you can quickly turn brochures and white papers into Kindle ebooks your clients can read and re-read in their spare moments. A series of these could tell all about your company and its services or products.

You probably have that series already sitting in your Marketing areas, formatted for big, glossy print magazines. Or a smaller bootstrap operation might have this material in its blog.

Consider that you could find many more clients when they are searching for solutions by Google or Amazon and come across your book. Then they get to the end of that book and find they can get more books in this series – *if they just become part of your mailing list.*

This is scalable from the smallest business just starting out, and also to the largest brick-and-mortar corporation.

And it takes little training to make ebooks (see the references linked in the Resources section below.)

A little more could get that ebook also printed as a nice, thin, informative piece suitable for handouts as a trade paperback.

Meanwhile, getting someone to record it gives you an additional resource any potential prospect could listen to while they were doing their exercise, or their daily commute (or even flying to their appointment with one of your sales team.)

This doesn't replace anything you are currently doing with your marketing. It just gives you additional marketing tools, and prospecting venues, so you can help your prospects find your contact information – via Amazon, of all places.

Consider this as you can. Download the podcast if you want.

Your choice. Have fun with it.

Sequence for Publishing a Short Read

1. Write it all out in a text editor (or get someone or some program to transcribe your audio.)

2. If it's over 2500 words, it's a candidate for an Amazon short read.

3. Do your first two proofs, then record your third proof. Send that text out for external proofing if you want. (Recommended, but optional.) Edit the audio into shape.

4. Import into LibreOffice for spellchecking (although Text-edit on the MAC does a decent job.)

5. Publish your podcast (using the text as show notes) and use IFTTT to syndicate it.

6. Create your ebook with a cover (in GIMP) and description, via Calibre.

7. Upload the ebook to Amazon as an original work.

8. Finalize your LibreOffice version and create a PDF from it.

9. Upload to CreateSpace as a book (provided it's over 32 pages in print, about 8,000 words - and you can pad it with ads for your other books if you want...)

10. Publish to Lulu:
a. As an ebook if you aren't opting for KDP exclusivity.
b. As a trade paperback - and order a proof to get their Expanded Reach option.

11. You can publish your book description to LinkedIn if it's a nice, long 4,000 character piece. Modify your cover for LI's art specs. By now you should have the Amazon link, so you can drop it in this your LinkedIn Pulse article.

12. Update your podcast with the links to your title's version.

Then start your next book, or get back to getting all your other ebooks published in hardcopy to increase your income even more.

The "Eyeball" Marketing Strategy for Self Published Books

(An excerpt from "Publish. Profit. Independence." - Available on Amazon and everywhere else.)

The simplicity of ebook sales can be simply stated:

Get Your eBook in Front of as Many Eyeballs as Possible.

But it's not all that simple.

Sure, there are at least 7 main outlets for ebooks. (And there's another 5 or 6 additional outlets as well...)

No one outlet has any given set of eyeballs in a monopoly. As a matter of fact, at no time can any one of them claim they have all ebook readers under their spell. The closest they can get is this paraphrase from old Abe Lincoln:

You can reach some of the readers most of the time,

You can reach most of the readers some of the time,

But no ebook outlet (or author) can reach most of the readers most of the time.

Added to this:

Poor marketers only try to reach some of the readers some of the time. (That's why they're still poor...)

How to reach as many eyeballs as possible

One trick in this is that **no given set of people agree on how they like their content served up to them**.

We are starting out with ebooks - most people would still rather read printed books. There's also audiobooks. With digital downloads, these are becoming ever more popular, especially for commutes. On top of that, there's also video versions that can be generated from the same audio. As well, the text can be converted to PDF's and slideshow presentations. And there are packages with combinations of all of these, like you can post on Bittorrent, as well as service providers such as iAmplify. Meanwhile, there is at least one ebook publisher who allows you to package A/V files with your ebook - Leanpub.

This gives a new twist to the old phrase: *Write Once, Publish Many Ways...*

- Write once,

- publish as many ways,

- in as many formats,

- to as many eyeballs

- as possible.

eBooks - The modern ebook author needs to realize that to reach the maximal amount of people viewing your work, you're going to have to be on all possible distribution lines - not just stick with Amazon. There's 6 other outlets who want to host your content - and they all reach different readers.

You want to translate (port) your text into multiple formats. Smashword ports your content to multiple formats - all written. epub, mobi, PDF, plus another half-dozen versions for different readers. Leanpub only covers PDF, ebub, mobi.

Audio - Then you have audiobooks. Of course, there's ACX which gets you into Audible, Amazon, iTunes. Better have your best show on there - they have serious quality standards. But you also have to realize that simple podcasts by the author are also in demand. Particularly as a bonus. iAmplify will host your media files, and add your PDF (or probably epub or other) as an afterthought. [*Update*: you can also post your audio book as "spoken word albums" and distribute through CDBaby...]

Video - iAmplify will also host your videos. Of course, you can put previews on the major and minor video sites as well. (Use your audio as a soundtrack, then add in powerpoint visuals built on the outline of your text.)

PDF's - For promotion, PDF previews can be posted on all the doc-sharing sites, which will bring your site traffic. Many powerpoint-viewing sites take PDF's as well.

Graphics - And then, there are always creating infographics to promote your content, based on the content itself. Pinterest, Flickr, etc. love these.

Your Bottom Line - The trick is to have your money-making backend sites and your promotional sites for generating traffic, search engine ranking, etc. There's going to be a balance.

This is again the whole point of writing. An avid fan base will boost sales and get the ebook outlet algorithms working in your favor.

By contrast, *low-selling ebooks are mostly condemned to that forgotten pile by those algorithms*, it seems especially with Amazon. All outlets have their own versions. Only Amazon really seems to value reviews, for instance. (Reviews have been proved to have little to do with actual purchase, higher is who originally told them about the book.) For my own use, out of 17 books posted to Amazon, the only ones which consistently sold were either .99 or free. But since Locke gamed their system, Amazon has been down on the 99 cent books. So – finally – *one* 99 cent book started taking off. A year later.

Meanwhile, I have *several* dozen books on other outlets (who aren't as restrictive on submissions) and know these same books routinely sell in good percentages. But no two outlets have the same audience. Some books I've put up on iTunes don't sell well on Kobo. I've got some books on Google Play which are accounting for about 50% of sales, while only 30% on iTunes, but less than a quarter of my sales occurring on Kobo. (And for a short while, one of my 99-cent public domain classics was favored by Kobo, which gave me a few hundred more in royalties - while it lasted.)

Backbench - The point in profitable publishing is to have a *deep* back-bench. The most successful authors have *dozens* of books up there.

I found that it's far more profitable to be a publisher than a writer. So I look for books which are under-marketed (which are easy to find in the public domain and in PLR) - then put them up with appealing covers and good descriptions, then publish them as widely as possible. Some sell well, others don't.

The trick is that for a few hours' work per book, I have quite a few which sell routinely for me. *And these will be selling for me from here on out.* I can then take these and market them further with additional versions, and Search Engine Marketing by providing a back-up website, previews on doc-sharing sites and Bittorrent, etc. I can also use that base popularity to generate extra sales by creating audiobooks and videos based on that proven seller.

Also, I can go back and review the non-sellers to see if something needs to be tweaked in their cover, description, or preview.

So that's my own algorithm, after a fashion.

It starts with having a ton of books up there, on as many outlets as possible, in as many formats as possible. This is now being expanded by being able to collect emails into lists, and offering that audience the alternative books they may have been missing. While this is still in its infancy, I can see this is the best route to leveraging all the above into some serious income.

Again, publishing pays more than writing. But the best writing will make publishing simpler and more profitable.

Remember: Eyeballs drive profits.

Resources and Links

(Visit http://calm.li/shortreadsmore
for links missing in the paperback edition.)

Audio available: http://livesensical.com/go/write-less/

Geoff Shaw's Udemy Courses

How to Succeed with Kindle Short Reads

Reverse Engineer Riveting Fiction and Write Best Selling Books

Mark Dawson's Facebook Advertising Course

Author-preneur Flipboard Magazine

Other books in this series

Visit http://livesensical.com/book-series/publishing-and-writing/

Available on Amazon, Lulu, and as Pay What You Want

Really Simple Writing & Publishing

Learn How to Write, Design, Format, Upload, and Sell Your Own Book for Low Cost or Free.

J'APE: Just Another Publicity Excuse

How to Publish Your (Kindle) Book for Shameless Self-Promotion and Profit

Publish. Profit. Independence.

How to Earn Extra Income and Financial Freedom by Publishing on Your Own

How to Write Less and Profit More

A Rich Adventure in Short Read Kindle Publishing - http://amzn.com/B01AQPPQM0

Writing Serial Fiction in the Real World

A Simple, Tongue-in-Cheek Guide to Writing and Publishing Episodic eBooks for Profit on Amazon (and Elsewhere.)

How to Help Librarians Fall in Love With Your Self-Published Book

...and Get More Sales When They Do.

Cracking the Kindle Sales Code

How to Search Engine Optimize Your Titles and Descriptions so Amazon Promotes Your Book and Recommends Buyers to You at No Cost

An Honest Kindle Booksales Blueprint

How to Break Out of the No-Sales Amazon Self-Publishing Basement and Start Routinely Earning Regular Passive Income From Your Kindle Booksales Without Added Expense or Tricks

Related Writing Texts Published by Midwest Journal Press

See: http://livesensical.com/go/writing-refs/

Carolyn Wells' *Mystery Story Technique for Writers*

Creating Your Children's Book by Thrive Learning Institute Library

Technique of Fiction Writing by Robert Saunders Dowst

Becoming the Fiction Storyteller of Your Dreams by Robert C. Worstell, Dorothea Brande, and Marie Shedlock

Disclaimer:

The author and publisher of this Ebook and the accompanying materials have used their best efforts in preparing this Ebook. The author and publisher make no representation or warranties with respect to the accuracy, applicability, fitness, or completeness of the contents of this Ebook. The information contained in this Ebook is strictly for educational purposes. Therefore, if you wish to apply ideas contained in this Ebook, you are taking full responsibility for your actions.

The author and publisher disclaim any warranties (express or implied), merchantability, or fitness for any particular purpose. The author and publisher shall in no event be held liable to any party for any direct, indirect, punitive, special, incidental or other consequential damages arising directly or indirectly from any use of this material, which is provided "as is", and without warranties.

As always, the advice of a competent legal, tax, accounting or other professional should be sought. The author and publisher do not warrant the performance, effectiveness or applicability of any sites listed or linked to in this Ebook. All links are for information purposes only and are not warranted for content, accuracy or any other implied or explicit purpose.

Lawyers are funny: Your mileage may vary. "Caution Contents May Be Hot."

Bonus

*Get No-Charge Access to
Writing and Publishing Materials
from Our Library Collection*

Instant Access – Join Here

Click or type into your browser:

http://livesensical.com/go/writingbooks/